Baseball Wisdom
from the Old Timers

Baseball Wisdom from the Old Timers

Margaret Queen

FOXGLOVE PRESS

On the Cover

Few sports icons have achieved the acclaim of the Louisville Slugger, the much-celebrated baseball bat first produced in the 1800s.

Young Bud Hillerich, an amateur baseball player who apprenticed in his father's woodworking shop, began making bats for himself and his teammates in 1880. From there, the stories diverge as to how the famous Slugger got its start. Some say Hillerich saw Pete "The Old Gladiator" Browning break his favorite bat in 1884 and made him a replacement. Others say Arlie Latham, a third baseman for the St. Louis Browns, broke a bat while playing in Louisville and sought out the Hilleriches's workshop. Either way, the company's reputation was solidified after Honus Wagner, a star for the Pittsburgh Pirates, signed a contract in 1905 as the first player ever to endorse a bat, followed by Ty Cobb in 1908.

Today, the legacy of wood bat production continues on West Main Street in Louisville, not far from the site of the original Hillerich wood-turning shop. The company produces more than a million bats a year.

Baseball Wisdom from the Old Timers by Margaret Queen

 Published by Foxglove Press
1-877-205-1932
© 2006 Foxglove Press

ISBN 1-882959-59-0

Design by Armour&Armour, Nashville, Tennessee

First Edition 2006
1 2 3 4 5 6 7 8 9 10

CONTENTS

Introduction   vii

The History of Baseball   2

Great Baseball Moments   7
     Enos Slaughter Steals to Win the '46 Series

Growing Up   8

All-Time Greats: Babe Ruth   10

The Power to Be Your Best   14

Managing to Win   16

Losing Hurts   23

All-Time Greats: Jackie Robinson   25

All-Time Greats: Willie Mays   28

Great Baseball Moments   30
     Willie Mays's Catch

The Manager-in-Chief   32

All-Time Greats: Ted Williams   36

Great Baseball Moments   38
     Ted Williams's Final At-Bat

Baseball Slang   40

A Man Walks into a Bar   45

All-Time Greats: Stan Musial   47

The Lighter Side   48

Great Baseball Moments   55
     Don Larsen's Perfect World Series Game

All-Time Greats: Frank Robinson   56

Love of the Game   58

All-Time Greats: Satchel Paige   62

Great Baseball Moments   66
     Johnny Vander Meer Pitches Two Consecutive No-Hitters

From the Bullpen   67

All-Time Greats: Sandy Koufax   76

CONTENTS

Great Baseball Moments   76
   Nolan Ryan Pitches His Seventh No-Hitter
All-Time Greats: Lou Gehrig   80
The Umpire Strikes Back   82
Great Baseball Moments   86
   Roger Maris's Sixty-First Home Run
Batter Up!   89
All-Time Greats: Mickey Mantle   92
Field of Dreams   97
Catcher in the Wry   98
All-Time Greats: Yogi Berra   100
Great Baseball Moments   104
   The Shot Heard 'Round the World
Baseball Talk   106
All-Time Greats: Joe DiMaggio   108
The Truth about Baseball   112
All-Time Greats: Ty Cobb   120
The Media is the Message   124
By the Numbers   125
All-Time Greats: Hank Aaron   126
Index   131
Sources   134

INTRODUCTION

Baseball is America's Game. The ball park is where we go to lose ourselves watching a game of skill and strategy. It is with great pride that we cheer on our home team. It is at the ball park where a family can enjoy the love of the game, and the pride in a team can be passed on from generation to generation. A hot dog seems to taste better here than anywhere else. How could you be from Boston or Chicago and not have a soft spot for the Red Sox or the Cubs? They represent our community pride and a sense of where we live and who we are.

The greatest thrill as a young child was to go to the ball park to root for our local team. My best friend's parents had box seats, and I was often invited to go the games with them. We would watch the players' every move, just hoping that a foul ball would come our way—the ultimate trophy from our evening at the ball park.

It may seem a little strange for a woman to be such a baseball fan. I grew up in a neighborhood of baseball players, and I was right in there with all the guys. We had a make-believe baseball team that had real practices every day. How many ten-year-old girls do you know who had her own catcher's mitt and chest protector and a full uniform?

I lived and breathed baseball. During the summer when school was out, I would listen to the professional ball games on the radio, holding a magazine with pictures of the players of each team. I could look at a picture of each batter as he stepped up to the plate. My most prized possession was a Larry Doby comic book, which I read a gazillion times.

My love of baseball continued through high school. I played shortstop on our varsity softball team for four years of high school, and my mitt still hangs on our living room wall with other sports memorabilia.

We can learn a lot from the old timers. They had great wisdom— laced with a sense of humor—to tell us about their love of the game.

—Margaret Queen

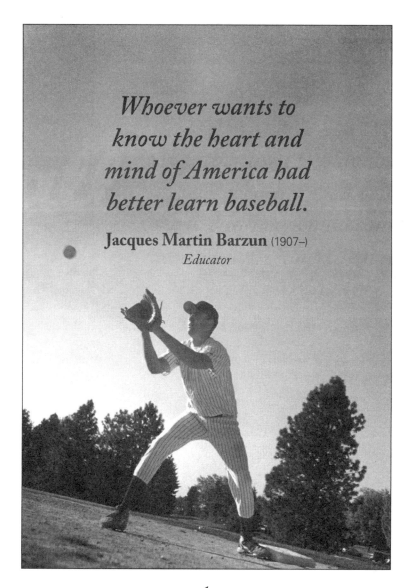

Whoever wants to know the heart and mind of America had better learn baseball.

Jacques Martin Barzun (1907–)
Educator

The History of Baseball

The game of baseball evolved from children's stick and ball games and the English game of rounders, a batting game first played in the eighteenth century.

The earliest written reference to the sport in America is a 1791 law prohibiting baseball play within eighty yards of the new meeting house in Pittsfield, Massachusetts. Newspaper articles from 1823 describe an organized game called "base ball" played in Manhattan.

Baseball grew in popularity in the early nineteenth century. Called townball, or base, or baseball, the game basically involved a batter hitting a pitched ball and running the bases (from one to five) without being tagged or "plugged"—hit by a ball thrown by a fielder.

Small towns began to form teams and big cities formed baseball clubs.

Father of Baseball

Popular legend says that Abner Doubleday invented the game, but baseball's true father is Alexander Cartwright. In 1845, Cartwright, of New York, wanted to create a standard list of rules by which all teams could compete. He established the modern baseball field and

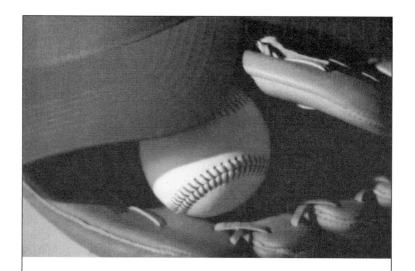

rules. Many of the original rules are still in play today, but in Cartwright's rules, plugging was allowed; a ball fielded on one bounce was an out; pitching was under-hand; and the game was won by the first team to score twenty-one "aces" (runs). In 1846, Cartwright's team, the Knickerbockers, lost to the New York Baseball Club in what is recognized as the first real baseball game.

Baseball became a popular leisure activity for wealthy young men. Soon soldiers in the Civil War were playing behind their lines. After the war they took the game back to their hometowns, where it was watched and played by Americans of every social status.

Professional baseball began in the United States around 1865. In 1869, The Cincinnati Red Stockings became the first all-professional team. The National League was founded in 1876. Several leagues formed and failed but the American League, created in 1893 as the Western League, succeeded. The best team in each league began playing in a World Series Championship in 1903.

Changes in the game

Baseball was a game of strategy in the early twentieth century. The "dead ball" era, which used an almost-soft ball, provided few home runs. For offense, the game relied on contact-hitters, bunting, and base stealing. In 1911, the game changed dramatically with the adoption of a ball with a cork center. Forty years of batting records began to fall, and the popularity of the game exploded.

Sportswriters were some of the game's key boosters. In the 1920s radio created a national, immediate audience for Babe Ruth's home run feats. Ruth revolutionized the game with his prowess as a home run hitter. He ushered in an era of economic prosperity for baseball, and became one of the most popular players in American history.

Breaking the segregation barrier

Baseball had never been a racially integrated sport, though a few African Americans played in the major leagues until segregation forced them out in the late 1880s. African-American ballplayers and businessmen organized their own touring teams, and formed the Negro Leagues. Some of the finest ballplayers played in these leagues, which reached their peak in popularity at the end of World War II. Major League Baseball's color barrier was finally broken when Jackie Robinson was signed by the National League's Brooklyn Dodgers in 1947. Since then, baseball has become fully integrated.

The middle of the twentieth century led baseball to the western United States. Pitching was dominant. Scoring was so low in the American League that the designated hitter was introduced; this rule now constitutes the major difference between the two leagues.

Most of the minor leagues collapsed in the 1950s and 1960s as televised baseball concentrated attention on the major leagues. Indoor stadiums, Astroturf, divisions within leagues, the designated hitter, World Series schedules, and lights at Wrigley Field were all created by the demands and power of television.

In spite of the popularity of baseball, the players became dissatisfied. They believed the owners had too much control. A series of strikes and lockouts began in baseball, affecting portions of the 1972 and 1981 seasons and culminating in the strike of 1994 that led to the cancellation of the World Series. The popularity of baseball diminished greatly as a result, and fans were slow to return.

Baseball enjoyed a resurgence in popularity in 1998 with the home run race between Mark McGwire and Sammy Sosa. The playoffs of 2004, highlighted by the Red Sox's comeback against the Yankees, resulted in what some have called a "New Golden Age" for baseball.

Baseball is an allegorical play about America, a poetic, complex, and subtle play of courage, fear, good luck, mistakes, patience about fate, and sober self-esteem.

Saul Steinberg (1914–1999)
Artist

Great Baseball Moments

ENOS SLAUGHTER STEALS TO WIN THE '46 SERIES

The St. Louis Cardinals enter the bottom of the eighth inning in the seventh game of the 1946 World Series against the Boston Red Sox. The game is tied 3-3. Enos Slaughter hits a leadoff single. After two outs, Slaughter is still on first. Harry Walker hits a single to left center and Slaughter runs. He rounds second, ignoring the third-base coach's signals to slide into third, and heads for home. The throw to home is off the mark and Slaughter slides into home for the ultimate Series winning run.

> He was one of the great hustlers of baseball. He loved baseball. He always ran hard and played hard.
> **Hall of Fame Teammate Stan Musial** (1920–)

My father used to play with my brother and me in the yard. Mother would come out and say, "You're tearing up the grass." My dad would reply, "We're raising boys."

Harmon Killebrew (1936–)
Minnesota Twins

My mother used to pitch to me and
my father would shag balls. If I hit one
up the middle close to my mother, I'd
have extra chores to do. My mother was
instrumental in making me a pull hitter.

Eddie Mathews (1931–2001)
Milwaukee Braves

You gotta be a man to play baseball
for a living, but you gotta have
a lot of little boy in you.

Roy Campanella (1921–1993)
Brooklyn Dodgers

"This is America," my father used to
say to me, "and in this country a smart
young fellow like you can grow up
and do just about anything." My dad,
no doubt, was thinking doctor, lawyer,
teacher, scientist, or businessman. I was
thinking second base, New York Yankees.

Joe Lieberman (1942–)
U.S. Senator from Connecticut

Babe Ruth

Elected to Hall of Fame	1936
Main Position	Right Field
Primary Team	New York Yankees

B abe Ruth is considered to be the best baseball player of all time. During his twenty-two year career, "The Sultan of Swat" was the most prolific home run hitter of his time.

George Herman Ruth did not have a happy childhood—he was schooled at St. Mary's, a Catholic reformatory. He found his pleasure in playing baseball.

His skill was noticed immediately when Ruth began pitching at age fifteen. He was signed by the Baltimore Orioles at age nineteen, and referred to as talent scout Jack Dunn's "newest babe." After that he was known as Babe.

After several months, the Boston Red Sox, for whom he pitched and played outfield for six years, bought his contract. He proved to be one of the game's best pitchers. He led the AL with a 1.75 ERA and nine shutouts in 1916, going 23-12 for the world champion Red Sox and won a career-high twenty-four games in 1917. And his batting average was .304—for a pitcher!

Ruth was sold to the Yankees in 1920, where he hit fifty-four home runs in 1920, fifty-nine in 1921, and sixty in 1927.

From 1926 through 1931, he averaged more than fifty home runs a year. No one has matched his slugging average (total bases divided by at-bats) of .847 in 1920, or his career record of .690. In 1927 he hit a record sixty home runs.

Ruth appeared in ten World Series, and was a larger-than-life character off the diamond as well. His charisma, ego, and carousing were legendary.

"The Great Bambino" retired in 1935 after hitting home run number 714.

Every strike brings me closer to the next home run.
Babe Ruth

(1895–1948)

Out of the Mouth of Babe

All ballplayers should quit when it starts
to feel as if all the baselines run uphill.

Babe Ruth (1895–1948)
New York Yankees

The way a team plays as a whole
determines its success. You may have the
greatest bunch of individual stars in the
world, but if they don't play together,
the club won't be worth a dime.

Babe Ruth (1895–1948)
New York Yankees

All I can tell 'em is I pick a good one
and sock it. I get back to the dugout and
they ask me what it was I hit and I tell
'em I don't know except it looked good.

Babe Ruth (1895–1948)
New York Yankees

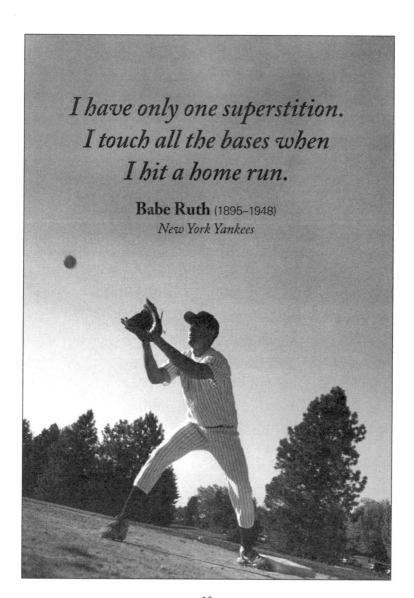

*I have only one superstition.
I touch all the bases when
I hit a home run.*

Babe Ruth (1895–1948)
New York Yankees

The Power to Be Your Best

Anything less would not have been
worthy of me. Anything more
would not have been possible.

Carl Yastrzemski (1939–)
Boston Red Sox

I owe the public just one
thing—a good performance.

Bob Gibson (1935–)
St. Louis Cardinals

Every day is a new opportunity.
You can build on yesterday's
success or put its failures
behind and start over again.
That's the way baseball is.

Bob Feller (1918–)
Cleveland Indians

The best ball player is the one who
doesn't think he made good. He
keeps trying to convince you.

Casey Stengel (1890–1975)
Manager, New York Yankees

You owe it to yourself to be the best you
can possibly be—in baseball and in life.

Pete Rose (1941–)
Cincinnati Reds, Philadelphia Phillies

When I was playing I never wished
I was doing anything else. I think
being a professional athlete is
the finest thing man can do.

Bob Gibson (1935–)
St. Louis Cardinals

I want to be remembered as a ball
player who gave all he had to give.

Roberto Clemente (1955–1972)
Pittsburgh Pirates

Managing to Win

If I were playing third base and my mother was rounding third with the run that was going to beat us, I'd trip her. Oh, I'd pick her up and brush her off and say, "Sorry, Mom" . . . but nobody beats me.

Leo Durocher (1905–1991)
Manager, Brooklyn Dodgers

The only bad thing about winning the pennant is that you have to manage the All-Star Game the next year. I'd rather go fishing for three days.

Whitey Herzog (1931–)
Manager, Kansas City Royals,
California Angels, St. Louis Cardinals

The key to winning baseball games is pitching, fundamentals, and three-run homers.

Earl Weaver (1930–)
Manager, Baltimore Orioles

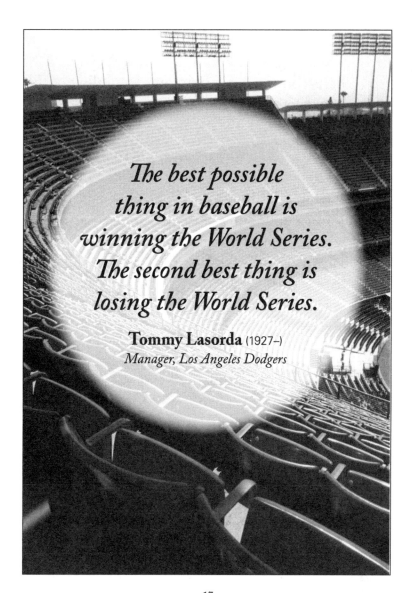

The best possible thing in baseball is winning the World Series. The second best thing is losing the World Series.

Tommy Lasorda (1927–)
Manager, Los Angeles Dodgers

Managing is like holding a dove in your hand. Squeeze too hard and you kill it; not hard enough, and it flies away.

Tommy Lasorda (1927–)
Manager, Los Angeles Dodgers

No matter how good you are, you're going to lose one-third of your games. No matter how bad you are, you're going to win one-third of your games. It's the other third that makes the difference.

Tommy Lasorda (1927–)
Manager, Los Angeles Dodgers

ON CASEY STENGEL: I'm probably the only guy who worked for Stengel before and after he was a genius.

Warren Spahn (1921–2003)
*Milwaukee Braves, winningest
left-handed pitcher of all time*

My best game plan is to sit on the
bench and call out specific instructions
like "C'mon Boog," "Get a hold of
one, Frank," or "Let's go, Brooks."

Earl Weaver (1930–)
Manager, Baltimore Orioles

Give me scratching, diving, hungry
ball players who come to kill you.

Leo Durocher (1905–1991)
Manager, New York Giants, Brooklyn Dodgers

Play every game . . . as if your job
depended on it. It just might.

Casey Stengel (1890–1975)
Manager, New York Yankees

I've always said I could manage Adolf Hitler,
Benito Mussolini, and Hirohito. That doesn't
mean I'd like them, but I'd manage them.

Billy Martin (1928–1989)
Manager, New York Yankees, New York Yankees,
New York Yankees, New York Yankees, New York Yankees

Baseball has been good to me
since I quit trying to play it.

Whitey Herzog (1931–)
Manager, Kansas City Royals,
California Angels, St. Louis Cardinals

Baseball is like driving; it's the one
who gets home safely that counts.

Tommy Lasorda (1927–)
Manager, Los Angeles Dodgers

It's easy to get the players; it's getting
them to play together that's the hard part.

Casey Stengel (1890–1975)
Manager, New York Yankees

ON CASEY STENGEL: Casey knew his
baseball. He only made it look like he
was fooling around. He knew every
move that was ever invented and some
that we haven't even caught on to yet.

Sparky Anderson (1934–)
Manager, Cincinnati Reds, Detroit Tigers

Managing is getting
paid for home runs
that someone else hits.

Casey Stengel (1890–1975)
Manager, New York Yankees

The secret to managing a
ball club is to keep the five
guys who hate you away from
the five who are undecided.

Casey Stengel (1890–1975)
Manager, New York Yankees

More than anyone else
Hank Aaron made me
wish I wasn't a manager.

Walter Alston (1911–1984)
Manager, Los Angeles Dodgers

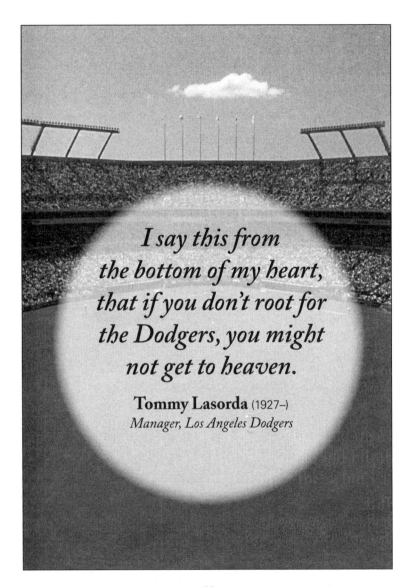

*I say this from
the bottom of my heart,
that if you don't root for
the Dodgers, you might
not get to heaven.*

Tommy Lasorda (1927–)
Manager, Los Angeles Dodgers

Losing Hurts

You can't tell how much spirit a
team has until it starts losing.

Rocky Colavito (1933–)
*Cleveland Indians, Detroit Tigers, Oakland As,
Chicago White Sox, Dodgers, New York Yankees*

The only way to prove you are
a good sport is to lose.

Ernie Banks (1931–)
Chicago Cubs

On my tombstone just write,
"The sorest loser that ever lived."

Earl Weaver (1930–)
Manager, Baltimore Orioles

Show me a good loser, and
I'll show you an idiot.

Leo Durocher (1905–1991)
Manager, New York Giants, Brooklyn Dodgers

All-Time Greats

Jackie Robinson

Elected to Hall of Fame	1962 (first African American)
Main Position	Second Base
Primary Team	Brooklyn Dodgers

Jackie Robinson will always be remembered as the player who truly broke the color barrier in major league baseball.

He was a basketball, football, track, and baseball star at UCLA—the first student to letter in four different sports. To enlist in the Army during WWII, Robinson left UCLA in 1942. He was refused entry to Officer Candidate School because of segregation. He fought for his right to attend, and was later accepted.

After an honorable discharge in 1944, he played ball for the Kansas City Monarchs of the Negro American League. In 1947, Robinson's debut with the Brooklyn Dodgers was a historic event, breaking the color barrier in baseball. He had a fiery temper, but learned to control it, as he had to endure racial harassment from both players and fans. He quickly became baseball's top drawing card and a symbol of hope to millions of Americans.

During his rookie season he played in 151 games, hit .297, and was league leader with twenty-nine stolen bases. He was awarded Rookie of the Year in 1947 and Most Valuable Player for the National League in 1949.

His determination and hustle were legendary, and in his prime every team respected him. Robinson was an exceptionally talented and disciplined hitter, with a career average of .311 and many more walks than strikeouts. With Robinson on board, the Dodgers won six pennants in his ten seasons. He dominated games on the base paths, stealing home nineteen times and aggravated opposing pitchers with his aggressive base running style.

Robinson retired on January 5, 1957.

A life is not important except in the impact it has on other lives.

Jackie Robinson (1919–1972)
Brooklyn Dodgers

ON JACKIE ROBINSON: With grace and steely determination, he pushed open a door that should never have been closed and held it open for the countless talented young men and women who followed.

Bill Clinton (1946–)
42nd President of the United States

Baseball is like a poker game. Nobody wants to quit when you're ahead.

Jackie Robinson (1919–1972)
Brooklyn Dodgers

The way I figure it, I was even with baseball and baseball with me. The game had done much for me, and I had done much for it.

Jackie Robinson (1919–1972)
Brooklyn Dodgers

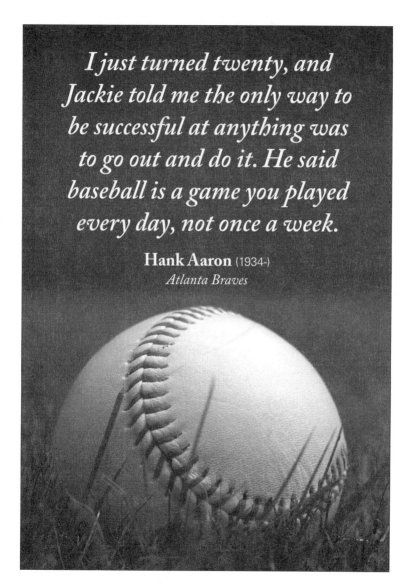

I just turned twenty, and Jackie told me the only way to be successful at anything was to go out and do it. He said baseball is a game you played every day, not once a week.

Hank Aaron (1934-)
Atlanta Braves

Willie Mays

Elected to Hall of Fame	1979
Main Position	Center Field
Primary Team	San Francisco Giants

Willie Mays's preeminence as a centerfielder is supported by his career total of 7,095 putouts, the most in Major League history.

Mays starred in baseball, basketball, and football in high school before joining the Birmingham Barons of the Negro National League at age seventeen. The New York Giants bought his contract in 1950, then he served in the army in 1952 and 1953.

Mays had a habit of addressing his fellow players with a high-spirited "say hey" salutation, prompting a New York sportswriter to nickname him the "Say Hey Kid." He became a folk hero in New York City by playing stickball with children in Harlem streets.

Along with Mickey Mantle and Hank Aaron, Mays was a dominant slugger of the 1950s and 1960s.

The Say Hey Kid played with enthusiasm and exuberance while excelling in all phases of the game—hitting for average and power, fielding, throwing, and base running. His career statistics include 3,283 hits and 660 home runs. The Giants superstar earned National League Rookie of the Year honors in 1951 and two MVP awards. He accumulated twelve Gold Gloves, played in a record-tying twenty-four All-Star games, and participated in four World Series.

When he retired as a player in 1973, Mays became a goodwill ambassador and part-time coach for the Mets, as well as a greeter for a local hotel casino.

I never dreamed
about being President;
I wanted to be
Willie Mays.

George W. Bush (1946–)
43rd President of the United States

Great Baseball Moments

WILLIE MAYS'S CATCH

It's the first game of the 1954 World Series between the New York Giants and the Cleveland Indians at the Polo Grounds. In the top of the eighth inning, Vic Wertz of the Indians hits a line drive to deep centerfield. Willie Mays runs and makes an incredible over-the-shoulder catch. Mays then throws a rocket to second base that keeps the lead runner from scoring. The Giants go on to win this exciting game.

No record book reflects this kind of concentration, determination, perseverance or ability. As a player, Willie Mays could never be captured by mere statistics.

Harry Jupiter
The San Francisco Chronicle

Willie Mays and his glove:
where triples go to die.

Fresco Thompson (1902–1968)
New York Giants

The Say-Hey Kid Said:

I think I was the best
baseball player I ever saw.

Willie Mays (1931–)
San Francisco Giants

I remember the last season I played.
I went home after a ballgame one
day, lay down on my bed, and tears
came to my eyes. How can you explain
that? You cry because you love her.
I cried, I guess, because I loved
baseball and I knew I had to leave it.

Willie Mays (1931–)
San Francisco Giants

They throw the ball, I hit it.
They hit the ball, I catch it.

Willie Mays (1931–)
San Francisco Giants

The Manager-in-Chief

Not making the baseball
team at West Point
was one of the greatest
disappointments of my
life, maybe my greatest.

Dwight D. Eisenhower (1890–1969)
34th President of the United States

I couldn't see well enough to
play when I was a boy, so they
gave me a specific job. They
made me an umpire.

Harry Truman (1884–1972)
33rd President of the United States

Good ballplayers
make good citizens.

Chester A. Arthur (1829–1886)
21st President of the United States

If I didn't have to hobble up those
steps in front of all those people, I'd
be out at that ball park every day.

Franklin Roosevelt (1882–1945)
32nd President of the United States

I never leave a game before the last pitch,
because in baseball, as in life and especially
politics, you never know what will happen.

Richard Nixon (1913–1994)
37th President of the United States

I had a life-long ambition to be
a professional baseball player, but
nobody would sign me up.

Gerald Ford (1913–)
38th President of the United States

I watch a lot of baseball on the radio.

Gerald Ford (1913–)
38th President of the United States

I just know that it's an ugly rumor
that Gaylord Perry and I are the only
two people left alive that saw Abner
Doubleday throw out the first pitch.

Ronald Reagan (1911–2004)
40th President of the United States

One of the great things about living
here [in the White House] is that you
don't have to sign up for a baseball
fantasy camp to meet your heroes.
It turns out, they come here.

George W. Bush (1946–)
43rd President of the United States

Next to religion, baseball has furnished
a greater impact on American life
than any other institution.

Herbert Hoover (1874–1964)
31st President of the United States

When I was a small boy in Kansas a friend of mine and I went fishing and we talked about what we wanted to do when we grew up. I told him that I wanted to be a real Major League baseball player. My friend said he wanted to be President of the United States. Neither of us got our wish.

Dwight D. Eisenhower (1890–1969)
34th President of the United States

Ted Williams

Elected to Hall of Fame	1966
Main Position	Left Field
Primary Team	Boston Red Sox
Managed	Washington Senators
	Texas Rangers

Ted Williams, one of baseball's greatest sluggers, was the last player to hit over .400, a feat he accomplished in 1941.

He played nineteen seasons with the Boston Red Sox, with a career batting average of .344 and 521 home runs.

He was self-conscious, shy, and sensitive growing up. With his parents rarely around, Ted spent his time in playgrounds. "I used to hit tennis balls, old baseballs, balls made of rags—anything," he said. "I didn't think I'd be a particularly good hitter, I just liked to do it."

After high school baseball and some minor league play, Williams started with the Boston Red Sox in 1939. In 1941 Williams ended the season with a batting average of .406.

Outspoken, talented, patriotic, demanding, larger than life: all apply to Ted Williams. He never got along with the baseball press. He had a mercurial temper, was distrustful of many of the trappings of stardom, and was always something of a loner. But for two decades, he was baseball's best hitter.

No one loved hitting more than Williams, who called hitting a pitch "the hardest single feat in sports." An intense student of batting, "The Splendid Splinter" wrote a book on the subject, *The Science of Hitting* in 1970, which is still studied today.

Williams was a two-time American League MVP winner, led the league in batting six times, and won the Triple Crown twice.

He retired from playing in 1960 after hitting a home run in his final at-bat. Then Williams surprised nearly everyone in baseball when in 1969 he became manager of the Washington Senators (now the Texas Rangers). Williams brought his first team in at 86-76, and was voted Manager of the Year.

After his retirement from managing in 1972, he became an avid sport fisherman, and hosted a television show about fishing. He has been inducted into the Fishing Hall of Fame.

Great Baseball Moments

TED WILLIAMS'S FINAL AT-BAT

In a game against the Baltimore Orioles in 1960, Ted Williams hits his 521st career home run in his final at bat before retirement. It is a fitting finish for the powerful "Splendid Splinter."

I've found that you don't need to wear a necktie if you can hit.

Ted Williams (1918–2002)

He [Ted Williams] was the best pure hitter I ever saw. He was feared.

Joe DiMaggio (1914–1999)
New York Yankees

The Splendid Splinter Said:

Whenever I went into a slump,
I went back to fundamentals.
Wait on the ball, be quick, use
a light bat, and choke up.

Ted Williams (1918–2002)
Boston Red Sox

Baseball is the only field
of endeavor where a man can
succeed three times out of ten and
be considered a good performer.

Ted Williams (1918–2002)
Boston Red Sox

All I want out of life is that when
I walk down the street folks will say,
"There goes the greatest
hitter that ever lived."

Ted Williams (1918–2002)
Boston Red Sox

Baseball Slang

Ballpark Figure: Rough estimate

Bases loaded: It's a crucial situation. Everything has been prepared; now it's time to deliver.

Bench clearer: A rowdy physical fight involving many players

Batting 1000: You're doing great!

Big show, big leagues (the show, the Major Leagues, the Majors): A big project—competing with others at a high level of competition

Bunt: Sometimes you can't make the big play and just have to do what it takes to get the job done

Bush or bush league: Unprofessional, inferior, or amateurish. Originally a reference to minor league baseball, implying that something is not ready for prime time

Can of corn: An easy accomplishment; an easy outfield catch

Caught off base, caught napping: Not ready for the next step of something; in jeopardy

Cover all the bases: Take care of all the details; prepare adequately

Clean-up hitter: Someone who comes in to take care of something started by others

Clutch or in the clutch: Performing well when it really counts

Curveball: A surprise, something unexpected

Designated hitter: It's up to you; the others couldn't get it done.

Drop the ball: Fail to get the job done

Fast ball: An idea that may not stand up over time; someone trying to sneak something by you

Get to first base: To succeed in the first step of something, such as a job interview

Go to bat for: Put your energies into a project or person

"Going, going, gone!": Dramatic description of anything that has departed

Grand slam: An excellent outcome (same as no-hitter)

Heavy hitter: Powerful person

Home field advantage: Having an event where you feel most comfortable

Home run (hit a home run, hit it out of the park, knock it out of the park): To completely succeed at something (opposite of strike out)

"It ain't over 'til it's over!": A Yogism (famous quotation from player Yogi Berra): Don't quit working on the job until it's completely finished.

Keep your eye on the ball: Keep focused on your task

Left field: Unusual, unexpected, or irrational

Line up: The agenda

No-hitter: Performing perfectly

Off base: Out of line, inappropriate behavior, working on faulty assumptions

On deck: Next in line, ready to participate

On the ball: Alert, focused

On the bench: waiting to participate

Out in left field: Strange, odd, not normal. An irrational observation. Also, describing a person with strange ideas

Out of his league: Can't compete with others at this level

Out of left field: An idea, claim or argument that is unexpected

Pinch hit: Stand in for someone else

Rain check: An invitation that may be renewed at a later date

Rained out: When an event is cancelled or postponed

Right off the bat: At the very beginning

Rookie: An individual who is new at something

Screwball: Strange, eccentric, crazy, or zany

Southpaw: A left-handed person

Step up to the plate: To rise to an occasion in life; ready to perform

Strike out: To fail completely at something

Switch-hitter, swings both ways: Bisexual

Three strikes, you're out: Three felonies and you get a life sentence

Throw a curve: Don't let them throw you a curve; be prepared, ready for anything

Walk: An acquittal given to a defendant in a criminal trial

Whiffleball, whiff, whiff out: Not even come close to solving the problem

Whole new ball game: A new, fresh start

A Man Walks into a Bar

A man walks into a bar with a dog. The bartender says, "You can't bring that dog in here."

"You don't understand," says the man. "This is no regular dog, he can talk."

"Listen, pal," says the bartender. "If that dog can talk, I'll give you a hundred bucks."

The man puts the dog on a stool, and asks him, "What's on top of a house?"

"Roof!"

"Right. And what's on the outside of a tree?"

"Bark!"

"And who's the greatest baseball player of all time?"

"Ruth!"

The bartender is furious. "Listen, pal," he says, "get out of here before I belt you."

As soon as they're on the street, the dog turns to the man and says, "Do you think I should have said 'DiMaggio'?"

Stan Musial

Elected to Hall of Fame	1969
Main Position	Left Field
Primary Team	St. Louis Cardinals

Stan Musial topped .300 seventeen times and won seven NL batting titles with his trademark closed batting stance and stinging line drives.

When he was seventeen, Musial started his career as a pitcher. After a shoulder injury, he moved to the outfield in 1940, and focused on hitting.

He spent part of his career serving in the Navy in WWII. But Musial was a Cardinal for twenty-two seasons, a team record. He played 1,890 games in the outfield, and 1,016 games at first base. He won the National League Most Valuable Player award in 1943, 1946, and 1948, and in 1957, received *Sports Illustrated* magazine's "Sportsman of the Year" award.

He was very consistent, at home or away. He studied different pitchers and was able to determine how their pitches would cross home plate. He was nicknamed

"The Man" by Dodger fans because of the havoc he wrought at Ebbets Field.

After his playing days were over, he served as general manager and senior vice president of the Cardinals for more than twenty-five years. His statue, in his left-handed batting crouch, stands in front of Busch Stadium. In St. Louis, he is a popular restaurateur and beloved city figure.

Few players have matched his accomplishments and consistency. Even fewer have garnered the admiration and affection of fans. He was not a showman, just an honest, hardworking player.

Stan Musial could hit .300
with a fountain pen.

Joe Garagiola (1926–)
*St. Louis Cardinals, Pittsburgh Pirates, Chicago Cubs,
New York Giants, sports broadcaster*

The Lighter Side

If it weren't for baseball, many
kids wouldn't know what a
millionaire looked like.

Phyllis Diller (1917–)
Comedian

The trouble is not that players
have sex the night before a game.
It's that they stay out all
night looking for it.

Casey Stengel (1890–1975)
Manager, New York Yankees

I've seldom seen a horny player
walk into a bar and not let out
exactly what he did for a living.

Johnny Bench (1947–)
Cincinnati Reds

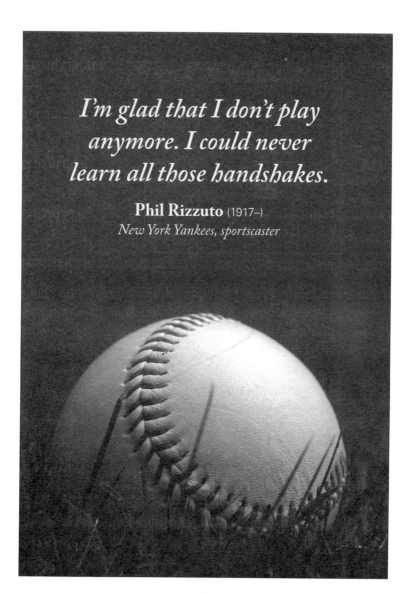

I'm glad that I don't play anymore. I could never learn all those handshakes.

Phil Rizzuto (1917–)
New York Yankees, sportscaster

Why does everybody stand
up and sing "Take Me Out
to the Ballgame," when
they're already there?

Larry Anderson (1952–)
Milwaukee Brewers, Chicago White Sox

A conceited new rookie
was pitching his first game. He
walked the first five men he faced
and the manager took him out of
the game. The rookie slammed his
glove on the ground as he yelled,
"Damn it, the jerk took me out
when I had a no-hitter going."

Author Unknown

The only thing worse than a Mets
game is a Mets double hitter.

Casey Stengel (1890–1975)
Manager, New York Yankees

Q: Why is it so hot at Phillies games?

A: **Because there's not a fan in the place.**

Q: Why is it so windy at Candlestick Park?

A: **Because of all the Giant fans!**

Q: What do you get when you cross a tree with a baseball player?

A: **Babe Root.**

Q: What takes longer, running from first base to second, or from second to third?

A: **Second to third, because you have to go through a shortstop.**

Q: Why did the baseball player
take his bat to the library?
A: **Because his teacher told
him to hit the books!**

Q: What runs around the
field but never wins?
A: **A fence!**

Q: How many Major League umpires
does it take to change a lightbulb?
A: **None, they just sit there
in the dark and bitch.**

Q: How can you tell when George
Steinbrenner is lying?
A: **His lips are moving.**

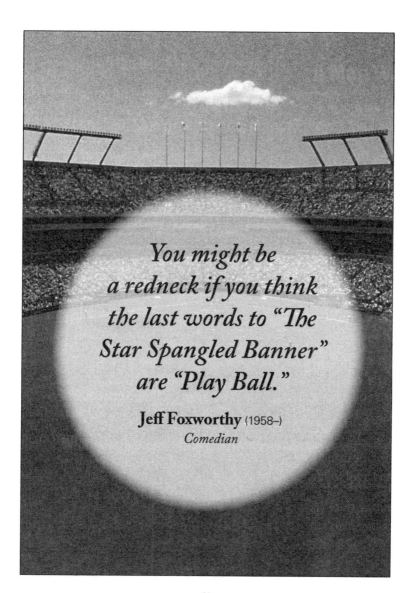

*You might be
a redneck if you think
the last words to "The
Star Spangled Banner"
are "Play Ball."*

Jeff Foxworthy (1958–)
Comedian

A man was visiting his oldest friend on his deathbed. "When you die," he said, "I want you to come back and tell me if there's baseball in heaven." A couple of days after his friend's death, he heard a ghostly voice. "I've got some good news and some bad," the voice said. "The good news is, yes, there is baseball in heaven. "The bad news is, you're pitching on Wednesday."

●

If a woman has to choose between catching a fly ball and saving an infant's life, she will choose to save the infant's life without even considering if there are men on base.

Dave Barry (1947–)
Humorist

Great Baseball Moments

DON LARSEN'S PERFECT WORLD SERIES GAME

In the fifth game of the 1956 World Series, New York Yankee Don Larsen pitches a perfect game against the Brooklyn Dodgers. The New York Yankees win their seventeenth world championship.

The million-to-one shot came in. Hell froze over . . . Don Larsen today pitched a no-hit, no-run game in a World Series. He did it with a tremendous assortment of pitches, that seemed to have five forward speeds, including a slow one that ought to have been equipped with back-up lights.

Shirley Povich (1905–1998)
The Washington Post

Frank Robinson

Elected to Hall of Fame	1982
Main Position	Right Field
Primary Team	Cincinnati Reds
Managed	Cleveland Indians,
	San Francisco Giants,
	Baltimore Orioles,
	Montreal Expos

Frank Robinson, the first player to win an MVP award in each league, had successful careers with the Cincinnati Reds, Baltimore Orioles, Los Angeles Dodgers, California Angels, and Cleveland Indians.

Frank, a star in high school, was drafted by Cincinnati in 1953. Three years later he was starring in the major leagues as Rookie of the Year. He developed a reputation as an aggressive outfielder and a hard-charging runner.

"The Judge" was the nickname he earned by calling team meetings to straighten out his teammates or help end a losing streak. He also spoke out on a variety of racially charged issues.

He was a member of the 1966 and 1970 Baltimore Orioles when they won the World Series. Robinson won the World Series MVP Award in 1966, and the American League Triple Crown. He won Most Valuable Player twice, in 1961 with the Reds and 1966 with the Orioles. Robinson amassed 586 home runs and ended his career with 2,943 hits.

Robinson's intelligence and leadership helped him become the first black manager of a major league baseball team, when he became a player/manager with Cleveland in 1975. He was awarded the American League Manager of the Year Award in 1989 for leading the Baltimore Orioles to an 87-75 record. He has managed in four decades, and in 2002 became manager of the Montreal Expos, now the Washington Nationals.

Pitchers did me a favor when they knocked me down. It made me more determined.

Frank Robinson (1935–)
Cincinnati Reds

Love of the Game

Baseball is more than a game
to me; it's a religion.

Bill Klem (1874–1951)
Hall of Fame player

Baseball is like church. Many
attend, but few understand.

Wes Westrum (1922–2002)
Chicago Cubs; manager, New York Mets

People ask me what
I do in winter when
there's no baseball. I'll
tell you what I do.
I stare out the window
and wait for spring.

Rogers Hornsby (1896–1963)
St. Louis Cardinals

I think about baseball when
I wake up in the morning. I think
about it all day, and I dream about
it all night. The only time I don't
think about it is when I'm playing.

Carl Yastrzemski (1939–)
Boston Red Sox

That's the true harbinger of
spring, not crocuses or swallows
returning to Capistrano, but the
sound of a bat on a ball.

Bill Veeck (1914–1987)
Baseball team owner

This is a game to be savored,
not gulped. There's time to
discuss everything between
pitches or between innings.

Bill Veeck (1914–1987)
Baseball team owner

The other sports are just
sports. Baseball is love.

Bryant Gumbel (1948–)
Sportscaster

When they start the game,
they don't yell, "Work ball."
They say, "Play ball."

Willie Stargell (1940–2001)
Pittsburgh Pirates

The new definition of a heathen is a
man who has never played baseball.

Elbert Hubbard (1856–1915)
Author

I'd walk through hell in a
gasoline suit to play baseball.

Pete Rose (1941–)
Cincinnati Reds, Philadelphia Phillies

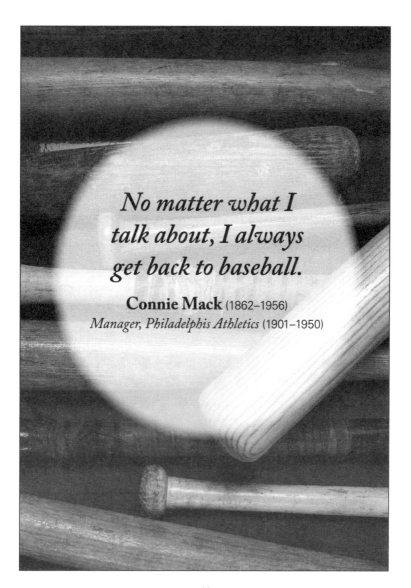

No matter what I talk about, I always get back to baseball.

Connie Mack (1862–1956)
Manager, Philadelphis Athletics (1901–1950)

Leroy "Satchel" Paige

Elected to Hall of Fame	1971
Main Position	Pitcher
Primary Team	Kansas City Monarchs

A tall, lanky, fireball thrower, Satchel Paige was arguably the Negro Leagues' hardest throwing pitcher, most colorful character, and greatest attraction. He earned his nickname "Satchel" by carrying bags for passengers at the railroad station when he was a boy in Alabama.

He was barred initially from the major leagues because he was African American, so he played in the Negro Leagues. He also honed his skills by traveling across the country and pitching for any team willing to meet his price. He sometimes traveled thirty thousand miles a year, and once pitched twenty-nine days consecutively.

Paige was a legendary storyteller and one of the most entertaining pitchers in baseball history. His goal was to play in the Major Leagues, and he finally got his chance when he joined the Cleveland Indians in 1948, one year after Jackie Robinson broke the color barrier in Major League baseball. He became the oldest player to make a Major League debut, and helped the Indians win the pennant.

Satchel will always be remembered for his longevity in the game, as he said, "Age is a question of mind over matter. If you don't mind, it doesn't matter." His career as a player spanned five decades. He also served as coach for the Atlanta Braves in 1968.

I ain't ever had a job.
I just play baseball.

Satchel Paige (1906–1982)
Kansas City Monarchs

ON SATCHEL PAIGE'S PITCHING:
It starts out like a baseball and when it gets to the plate, it looks like a marble.

Hack Wilson (1900–1948)
Chicago Cubs

Satchel Said:

Just take the ball and throw it
where you want to. Throw strikes.
Home plate don't move.

Satchel Paige (1906–1982)
Kansas City Monarchs

Never let your head hang down.
Never give up and sit down
and grieve. Find another way.
And don't pray when it rains if
you don't pray when the sun shines.

Satchel Paige (1906–1982)
Kansas City Monarchs

How old would you be if you
didn't know how old you was?

Satchel Paige (1906–1982)
Kansas City Monarchs

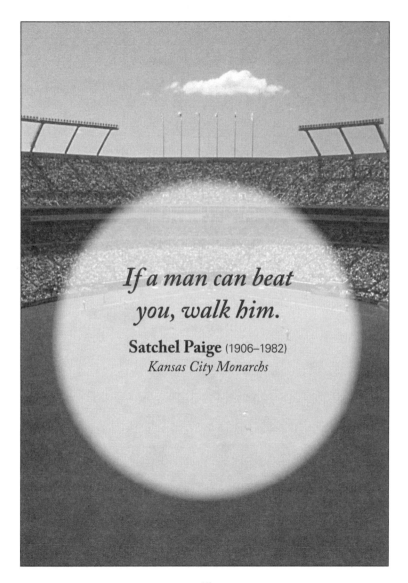

If a man can beat you, walk him.

Satchel Paige (1906–1982)
Kansas City Monarchs

Great Baseball Moments

VANDER MEER PITCHES TWO CONSECUTIVE NO-HITTERS

In a 1938 game with the Boston Bees, Cincinnati Reds pitcher Johnny Vander Meer pitches a no-hitter. Four days later, in their next game against the Dodgers, Vander Meer pitches his second straight no-hitter to make baseball history.

> All the publicity, the attention, the interviews, the photographs, were too much for me.
>
> **Johnny Vander Meer** (1914–1997)

From the Bullpen

I hate all hitters. I start a game mad
and I stay that way until it's over.

Don Drysdale (1936–)
Los Angeles Dodgers

My own little rule was two for one. If one
of my teammates got knocked down, then
I knocked down two on the other team.

Don Drysdale (1936–)
Los Angeles Dodgers

When I throw a curve that hangs and goes
for a hit, I want to chew up my glove.

Don Drysdale (1936–)
Los Angeles Dodgers

The pitcher has to find out if the hitter
is timid. And if the hitter is timid, he
has to remind the hitter he's timid.

Don Drysdale (1936–)
Los Angeles Dodgers

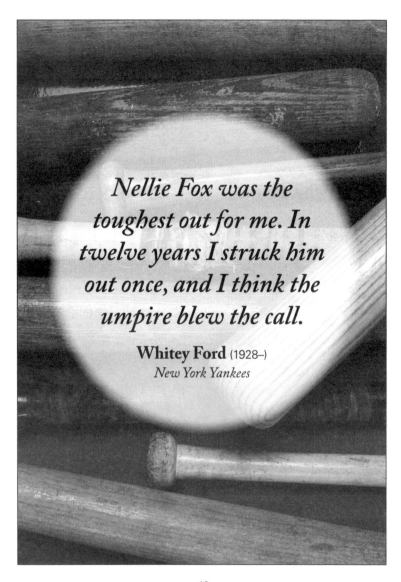

Nellie Fox was the toughest out for me. In twelve years I struck him out once, and I think the umpire blew the call.

Whitey Ford (1928–)
New York Yankees

You don't save a
pitcher for tomorrow.
Tomorrow it may rain.

Leo Durocher (1905–1991)
Manager, New York Giants, Brooklyn Dodgers

ON THROWING THE SPITBALL:
Let them think
I throw it, that gives me
an edge because it's
another pitch they
have to worry about.

Lew Burdett (1926–)
New York Yankees

A pitcher needs two
pitches: one they're
looking for and one
to cross them up.

Warren Spahn (1921–2003)
*Milwaukee Braves, winningest
left-handed pitcher of all time*

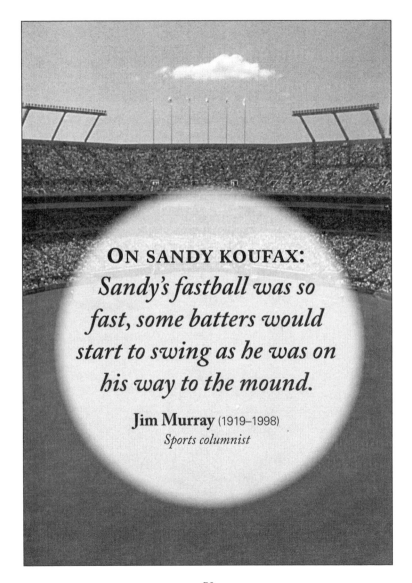

ON SANDY KOUFAX:

Sandy's fastball was so fast, some batters would start to swing as he was on his way to the mound.

Jim Murray (1919–1998)
Sports columnist

You can't sit on a lead and run a few
plays into the line and just kill the
clock. You've got to throw the ball over
the damned plate and give the other
man a chance. That's why baseball
is the greatest game of them all.

Earl Weaver (1930–)
Manager, Baltimore Orioles

Pro-rated at five hundred at-bats per
year, my 1.081 strike-outs would mean
that for two years out of the fourteen
I've played, I never touched the ball.

Norm Cash (1934–)
Chicago White Sox, Detroit Tigers

When I gave up a grand slam
to Pete LaCock, I knew
it was time to quit.

Bob Gibson (1935–)
St. Louis Cardinals

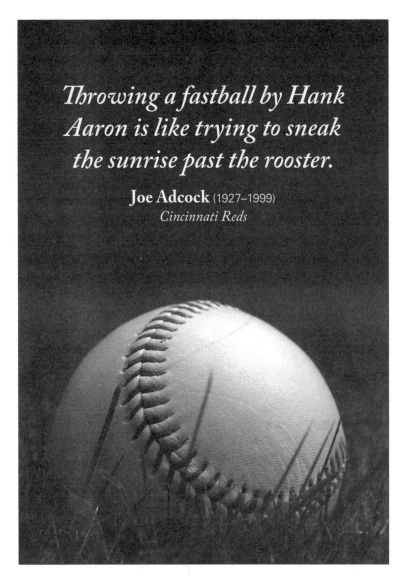

Throwing a fastball by Hank Aaron is like trying to sneak the sunrise past the rooster.

Joe Adcock (1927–1999)
Cincinnati Reds

The two most important things in my life
are good friends and a strong bullpen.

Bob Lemon (1920–)
Cleveland Indians

ON HIS 1974 ARM SURGERY: When they
operated, I told them to put in a Koufax
fastball. They did, but it was Mrs. Koufax's.

Tommy John (1943–)
New York Yankees

I would rather beat the Yankees
regularly than pitch a no-hit game.

Bob Feller (1918–)
Cleveland Indians

The dumber a pitcher is, the
better. When he gets smart and
begins to experiment with a lot of
different pitches, he's in trouble.

Dizzy Dean (1910–1974)
St. Louis Cardinals, Chicago Cubs

Future Baseball Star

A little boy was overheard talking to himself as he strutted through the backyard, wearing his baseball cap and toting a ball and bat:

"I'm the greatest hitter in the world," he announced. Then, he tossed the ball into the air, swung at it, and missed.

"Strike one!" he yelled. Undaunted, he picked up the ball and said again, "I'm the greatest hitter in the world!"

He tossed the ball into the air. When it came down he swung again and missed.

"Strike two!" he cried.

The boy then paused a moment to examine his bat and ball carefully.

He spit on his hands and rubbed them together. He straightened his cap and said once more, "I'm the greatest hitter in the world!"

Again he tossed the ball up in the air and swung at it. He missed.

"Strike three!"

"Wow!" he exclaimed. "I'm the greatest pitcher in the world."

I remember one time going out to
the mound to talk with Bob Gibson.
He told me to get back behind the
batter. The only thing I knew about
pitching was that it was hard to hit.

Tim McCarver (1942–)
St. Louis Cardinals

Back then, if you had a sore arm, the
only people concerned were you and
your wife. Now it's you, your wife, your
agent, your investment counselor, your
stock broker, and your publisher.

Jim Bouton (1939–)
New York Yankees

ON SATCHEL PAIGE: If Satch and I
were pitching on the same team, we'd
cinch the pennant by July 4 and go
fishing until World Series time.

Dizzy Dean (1910–1974)
Chicago Cubs, St. Louis Cardinals

Sandy Koufax

Elected to Hall of Fame	1972
Main Position	Pitcher
Primary Team	Los Angeles Dodgers

A fastball and devastating curve enabled Sandy Koufax to pitch no-hitters in four consecutive seasons, ending with a perfect game in 1965.

As a young man, his first love was basketball and he was a walk-on for the freshman basketball team at the University of Cincinnati. He decided to try out for the baseball team because of interesting trips they took on spring break. He threw the ball so hard that several catchers quit, and he made the varsity baseball team.

Koufax signed with the Dodgers after tryouts with several professional teams. After taming his blazing fastball, he enjoyed a five-year stretch as one of the most dominating pitchers in history. A notoriously difficult pitcher to hit against, he was the first Major Leaguer to pitch more than three no-hitters. Three seasons he won twenty-five games, he captured five straight ERA titles, and set a new record with 382 strikeouts in 1965. He posted a 0.95 ERA in four career World Series, leading the Dodgers to three championships.

Traumatic arthritis in his elbow forced Koufax to retire at the peak of his career at age thirty-one. At age thirty-six he became the youngest person ever elected to the Baseball Hall of Fame.

Show me a guy who can't pitch inside and I'll show you a loser.

Sandy Koufax (1935–)
Los Angeles Dodgers

A guy throws what he intends to throw; that's the definition of a good pitcher.

Sandy Koufax (1935–)
Los Angeles Dodgers

Pitching is the art of instilling fear.

Sandy Koufax (1935–)
Los Angeles Dodgers

Great Baseball Moments

NOLAN RYAN PITCHES HIS SEVENTH NO-HITTER

On May 1, 1991, forty-four-year-old Nolan Ryan of the Texas Rangers pitches his record seventh no-hitter in a game against the Toronto Blue Jays. No other pitcher has pitched more than four no-hitters in his career.

He's baseball's
exorcist, scares
the devil out of you."

Dick Sharon (1950–)
Detroit Tigers

Hitting is timing. Pitching is upsetting timing.

Warren Spahn (1921–2003)
Milwaukee Braves, winningest left-handed pitcher of all time

Lou Gehrig

Elected to Hall of Fame	1939
Main position	First Base
Primary Team	New York Yankees

Lou Gehrig's .361 batting average in seven World Series led the Yankees to six titles.

A gifted athlete, he received a football scholarship to Columbia to study engineering, but was banned from intercollegiate sports his freshman year because he played summer professional baseball under an assumed name.

Lou played fullback at Columbia in 1922, and then pitched and played first base for Columbia in 1923. A New York Yankees scout signed him to the Yankees in 1923 with a $1,500 bonus. He hit .423 in twenty-six at-bats that September for the Hartford team.

He became a major league Yankee in 1925 and didn't leave the playing field for more than thirteen years—playing in 2,130 consecutive games. His endurance and strength garnered him the nickname "Iron Horse."

After batting .295 in 1925, in 1926 Gehrig hit .313 and led the league with twenty triples. This was the first of twelve consecutive years that his average would top .300.

The Iron Horse had thirteen consecutive seasons with both 100 runs scored and 100 RBIs, averaging 139 runs and 148 RBIs, set an American League mark with 184 RBIs in 1931, hit a record twenty-three grand slams, and won the 1934 Triple Crown.

Gehrig died in 1941 of amyotrophic lateral sclerosis (ALS), now called Lou Gehrig's disease. He will always be remembered as humble, kind, and a tremendously talented athlete.

The Umpire Strikes Back

Umpire's heaven is a
place where he works
third base every game.
Home is where
the heartache is.

Ron Luciano (1937–1995)
Umpire

It ain't nothin'
'til I call it.

Bill Klem (1874–1951)
"Father of baseball umpires"

In a way, an umpire is
like a woman. He makes
quick decisions, never reverses
them, and doesn't think you're
safe if you are out.

Larry Goetz
Umpire

Fix your eye on the ball from the moment
the pitcher holds it in his glove. Follow
it as he throws to the plate and stay
with it until the play is complete. Action
takes place only when the ball goes.

Bill Klem (1874–1951)
"Father of baseball umpires"

The best umpired game is the game
in which the fans cannot recall the
umpires who worked it. If they don't
recognize you, you can enjoy your
dinner knowing you did a perfect job.

Bill Klem (1874–1951)
"Father of baseball umpires"

I sometimes get birthday cards
from fans. But its often the same
message—they hope it's my last.

Al Norman
Umpire

I never questioned the integrity of
an umpire. Their eyesight, yes.

Leo Durocher (1905–1991)
Manager, New York Giants, Brooklyn Dodgers

The job of arguing with the umpire
belongs to the manager, because
it won't hurt the team if he gets
thrown out of the game.

Earl Weaver (1930–)
Manager, Baltimore Orioles

You argue with the umpire because there
is nothing else you can do about it.

Leo Durocher (1905–1991)
Manager, New York Giants, Brooklyn Dodgers

Managers only argue on days
which end in the letter "Y."

Ron Luciano (1937–1995)
Umpire

One day the Devil challenged
the Lord to a baseball game.
Smiling, the Lord proclaimed,
"You don't have a chance;
I've got Babe Ruth, Mickey
Mantle, and all the greatest
players up here."
"Yes," laughed the Devil,
"But I have all the umpires."

Author Unknown

Great Baseball Moments

ROGER MARIS'S SIXTY-FIRST HOME RUN

In the final game of the 1961 season, New York Yankee Roger Maris hits his sixty-first home run of the season, breaking Babe Ruth's previous record.

1961: The year a record was broken, hearts were broken, and a man's life was changed forever. Roger Maris will forever be known as the man that took Babe Ruth's record. The man that changed the record books. Maris was hated, booed, cussed, and generally abused by the press and fans for his chase of the most well-known mark in all of baseball: Babe Ruth's sixty single-season home runs.

Maris began the year as just another hard-hitting Yankee. If anyone, his battery mate and media darling Mickey Mantle was scheduled to be the one to take over the spot on the all-time homer list. "Mick" was loved by the fans and the press, Maris was not. In fact, whenever Maris hit one of his home runs, he was quickly reminded that it was only because Mantle was behind him that he even saw a good pitch to hit. In fact, Maris spent his entire record-setting year cast as the villain in a media soap opera, while his good friend,

Mantle, was seen as the good guy whose own teammate was trying to steal his thunder.

Maris suffered greatly during the season. He actually lost his hair and had his and his family's lives threatened. The most heartbreaking part of his 1961 saga came after his record-breaking long ball. Baseball Commissioner Ford Frick decided that Maris' record would not stand against Ruth's because it was not done during the same number of games. The record was followed by the most famous asterisk in history. Maris could not take the pride he deserved in his great achievement. Speaking in 1980 he said: "They acted as though I was doing something wrong, poisoning the record books or something. Do you know what I have to show for sixty-one home runs? Nothing. Exactly nothing." What should have been one of baseball's greatest achievements became one of its saddest stories.

ON ROGER MARIS'S SIXTY-FIRST HOME RUN: When he hit it, he came into the dugout and they were all applauding. I mean, this is something that's only happened once in baseball, right? And the people were all applauding. They wanted him to come back out. He wouldn't come out, so the players had to push him back out. They forced him to come out and take a bow. That's the kind of guy he was. He was great, and I really liked him.

Mickey Mantle (1931–1995)
New York Yankees

Batter Up!

If I had my career to play over, one
thing I'd do differently is swing more.
Those twelve hundred walks I got . . .
nobody remembers them.

Pee Wee Reese (1918–1999)
Brooklyn Dodgers

The greatest thrill in the world is to
end the game with a home run and
watch everybody else walk off the field
while you're running the bases on air.

Al Rosen (1924–)
Cleveland Indians

All small men, all non-power
hitters, must learn to bunt well.
It's half your game.

Nellie Fox (1927–1975)
Chicago White Sox

When Neil Armstrong set
foot on the moon, he found
a baseball that Jimmie Foxx
hit off me in 1927.

Lefty Gomez (1908–1989)
New York Yankees

I have observed that baseball
is not unlike war, and when you
come right down to it, we
batters are heavy artillery.

Ty Cobb (1886–1961)
Detroit Tigers

If I stay healthy, I have a
chance to collect three
thousand hits and one
thousand errors.

George Brett (1953–)
Kansas City Royals

James "Cool Papa" Bell was
so fast, one time he hit a line
drive right back past my ear. I
turned around and saw the ball
hit his ass sliding into second.

Satchel Paige (1906–1982)
Kansas City Monarchs

The key to hitting is to relax,
concentrate, and don't hit
the ball to center field.

Stan Musial (1920–)
St. Louis Cardinals

When a pitcher's throwing
a spit ball, don't worry and
don't complain, just hit the
dry side like I do.

Stan Musial (1920–)
St. Louis Cardinals

Mickey Mantle

Elected to Hall of Fame	1974
Main Position	Centerfield
Primary Team	New York Yankees

No player in history has hit the ball farther than Mickey Mantle. He hit a 565-foot homer in 1953 and a 643-footer in 1960.

Mantle's father, a semi-pro player and huge baseball fan, named Mickey after a Hall of Fame catcher. As soon as he was old enough, his father and grandfather pitched to him daily, teaching him to be a switch-hitter. Working in the lead mines during the summers and doing farm chores helped develop his strength.

Mantle was a gifted athlete and played baseball, football, and basketball in high school.

At sixteen he played with a local semi-pro team, the Baxter Springs Whiz Kids. A Yankee scout wanted to sign him immediately, but when he found out he was only sixteen, he told Mickey he would come back when he graduated.

Mickey was signed to a minor league contract upon his graduation in 1949. Mickey went on to play with the Yankees' Class C team. In 1951, he went to spring training with the Yankees in Arizona, where manager Casey Stengel was amazed by his speed—2.9 seconds from home to first base.

In spite of several injuries, Mickey played more games as a Yankee than any other player (2,401). He won three Most Valuable Player awards ('56, '57, '62), and the Triple Crown in 1956 with a .353 average, 52 homers and 130 RBIs (leading the Major Leagues in all categories). Mantle appeared in twelve World Series during his first fourteen years with the Yankees, winning seven world championships. He still has World Series records with 18 home runs, 42 runs, 40 RBIs, and 43 bases on balls. He hit 536 career home runs and had a .298 career average.

After retiring in 1969, he opened Mickey Mantle's, a very popular restaurant in New York City.

If I knew I was going to be living this long,
I would have taken better care of myself.

Mickey Mantle (1931–1995)
New York Yankees

Mickey Said:

My dad taught me to switch hit. He and my grandfather, who was left-handed, pitched to me every day after school in the backyard. I batted lefty against my dad and righty against my granddad.

Mickey Mantle (1931–1995)
New York Yankees

Hitting the ball was easy; running around the bases was the tough part.

Mickey Mantle (1931–1995)
New York Yankees

After I hit a home run I had a habit of running the bases with my head down. I figured the pitcher already felt bad enough without me showing him up rounding the bases.

Mickey Mantle (1931–1995)
New York Yankees

Mickey Mantle meant an awful lot to me. He was a tremendous athlete. People didn't understand him the way they should have. He played ten years on one leg. But more than that, he was a tremendous person.

Hank Aaron (1934–)
Atlanta Braves

During my eighteen years,
I came to bat almost ten
thousand times. I struck out
about seventeen hundred times.
You figure a ball player will average
five hundred at-bats a season.
That means I played seven years
without ever hitting the ball.

Mickey Mantle (1931–1995)
New York Yankees

ON MICKEY MANTLE:
I played with him for nine years
and marveled at how hard he hit
and how fast he ran. How can
anyone forget the catch he made
on Gil Hodges's line drive to save
Don Larson's perfect game?

Tony Kubek (1936–)
New York Yankees

Field of Dreams

Every player should be accorded the
privilege of at least one season with
the Chicago Cubs. That's baseball as
it should be played—in God's own
sunshine. And that's really living.

Alvin Dark (1922–)
New York Giants, St. Louis Cardinals

Putting lights in Wrigley Field
is like putting aluminum siding
on the Sistine Chapel.

Roger Simon (1948–)
Journalist

A hot dog at the ballpark is better
than a steak at the Ritz.

Humphrey Bogart (1899–1957)
Actor

Catcher in the Wry

ON CHRIS CANNIZZARO: He's a remarkable catcher, that Canzoneri. He's the only defensive catcher in baseball who can't catch.

Casey Stengel (1890–1975)
Manager, New York Yankees

A catcher must want to catch. He must make up his mind that it isn't the terrible job it is painted, and that he isn't going to say every day, "Why, oh why, with so many other positions in baseball did I take up this one?"

Bill Dickey (1907-1993)
New York Yankees

I really want to be known more as a defensive guy, and take my pitchers to the next level. Every time I go out on the field, I take a lot of pride in what I do at the plate, but I take a lot more pride in what I do behind the plate.

Jorge Posada (1971–)
New York Yankees

Two hundred million Americans, and
there ain't two good catchers among them.

Casey Stengel (1890–1975)
Manager, New York Yankees

A catcher and his body are like
the outlaw and his horse. He's got
to ride that nag until it drops.

Johnny Bench (1947–)
Cincinnati Reds

No baseball pitcher would be worth
a darn without a catcher who
could handle the hot fastball.

Casey Stengel (1890–1975)
Manager, New York Yankees

The best way to catch a knuckleball
is to wait until the ball stops
rolling and then pick it up.

Bob Uecker (1935–)
*Milwaukee Braves, St. Louis Cardinals,
Philadelphia Phillies, Atlanta Braves*

Yogi Berra

Elected to Hall of Fame	1972
Main Position	Catcher
Primary Team	New York Yankees
Managed	New York Yankees, New York Mets

Lawrence Peter "Yogi" Berra was a brilliant catcher and dominant hitter during his nineteen-year career with the New York Yankees, becoming one of the most popular players in major league history. He got his nickname "Yogi" from a childhood friend who thought he looked like a Hindu holy man they had seen in a movie.

When he was eighteen, he joined the Navy and served in World War II. After the war, he played minor league ball and was called to the Major Leagues in 1946, beginning his career with the Yankees.

Yogi was a wild swinger at bat and was very difficult to strike out. When catching behind the plate, he was always talking—trying to distract the hitters. Berra was named to the American League All-Star team every year from 1948 to 1962. He topped the 100-RBI mark four years in a row and became a three-time American League MVP in a career that featured fourteen league pennants and ten World Series championships.

Following his playing career, Yogi continued in baseball as a manager and coach for several teams including the Yankees, New York Mets, and Houston Astros. Yogi is one of only a few managers to have won pennants in both the American and National Leagues.

A fan favorite and cultural icon, Berra, (who has a cartoon character, Yogi Bear, named for him), is famous for his "Yogisms," or interesting phrases, such as:

It ain't over 'til it's over.

It's like déjà vu all over again.

I didn't really say everything I said.

*Ninety percent of this game is mental,
and the other half is physical.*

Yogi's Wisdom

It ain't like football. You can't
make up no trick plays.

Yogi Berra (1925–)
New York Yankees

Slump? I ain't in no slump . . .
I just ain't hitting.

Yogi Berra (1925–)
New York Yankees

Little League baseball is a good thing
'cause it keeps the parents off the streets
and keeps the kids out of the house.

Yogi Berra (1925–)
New York Yankees

A nickel ain't worth a dime anymore.

Yogi Berra (1925–)
New York Yankees

Half the lies they tell about me aren't true.

Yogi Berra (1925–)
New York Yankees

A couple of Yogi Berra's teammates on the Yankees ball club swear that one night the stocky catcher was horrified to see a baby toppling off the roof of a cottage across the way from him. Yogi dashed over and made a miraculous catch—but then force of habit proved too much for him. He straightened up and threw the baby to second base.

Author Unknown

Great Baseball Moments

THE SHOT HEARD 'ROUND THE WORLD

In 1951 the New York Giants tie the Brooklyn Dodgers in regular season play and are forced to a best-of-three game playoff for the National League pennant.

With the playoff tied at one each, the Dodgers take a three-run lead in crucial Game Three. In the bottom of the ninth inning, the Giants score one run, and put two on base. Third baseman Bobby Thomson then comes up to bat.

Dodgers manager Chuck Dresen removes pitcher Don Newcombe and puts in reliever Ralph Branca. He throws one strike. Then on his next pitch, an inside fastball, Thomson slams it toward left field. It clears the high wall of the Polo Grounds and lands inside the lower deck.

With this triumphant home run, the Giants win the 1951 National League pennant.

ON BOBBY THOMSON'S HOME RUN:

Now it is done. The story ends.
And there is no way to tell
it. The art of fiction is dead.
Reality has strangled invention.
Only the utterly impossible,
the inexpressibly fantastic,
can ever be plausible again.

Red Smith (1905–1982)
Sports journalist

Baseball Metaphors

Baseball terms easily find their way into our everyday life. We often hear people say:

They *strike out* when they fail at something.

They *hit a home run* when they succeed at a difficult task.

They *step up to the plate* when they attempt to do something difficult.

Someone *throws you a curveball* when something unexpected happens.

And many more.

The most interesting use of baseball terms that I heard lately came at the confirmation hearing for Judge John Roberts before the Senate Judiciary Committee. He was talking about the fact that judges just enforce and interpret the laws rather than make the laws. Judge Roberts stated that "Judges are umpires. . . . My job is to call balls and strikes, not to pitch or bat." I was amused to hear the next morning on CNN correspondent Bob Franken say that he was sure the senators quizzing Judge Roberts would have a few curveballs and even a beanball in their arsenal of questions to Judge Roberts the next day. Using these baseball terms brought a little humor to this occasion.

My Favorite Quote

My favorite quote using baseball terms off the field comes from Barry Switzer, former head football coach at the University of Oklahoma (my alma mater).

Some people are born on third base and go through life thinking they hit a triple.

I've known a few of these people.

—Margaret Queen

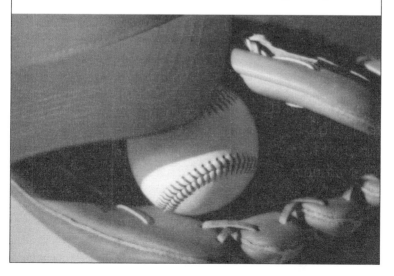

All-Time Greats

Joe DiMaggio

Elected to Hall of Fame	1955
Main Position	Center field
Primary Team	New York Yankees

In 1941, Joe DiMaggio hit safely in fifty-six straight games, a record that still stands as one of the biggest accomplishments in baseball history.

A high school dropout, DiMaggio began playing baseball for the San Francisco Seals in the Pacific Coast League, where in 1933 he batted safely in sixty-one consecutive games.

He joined the New York Yankees in 1936 and set American League rookie records for 132 runs, fifteen triples, twenty-nine home runs, 125 RBIs, with a .323 average.

DiMaggio was a leader, steering the Yankees to nine world championships. He was a graceful hitter with enormous power and strength, as well as an exceptional outfielder with a great throwing arm. Personally, DiMaggio was quiet, undemonstrative, introspective, and sometimes even stoic.

DiMaggio had two major league careers, one before World War II and the other after it. In each year of the former (1936–1942) he hit over .300 and exceeded 100 RBI.

In thirteen seasons he amassed 361 homers, averaged 118 RBIs annually and compiled a .325 lifetime batting average, and struck out only 369 times. He won two batting crowns and three MVP awards. At baseball's 1969 Centennial Celebration, he was named the game's greatest living player.

There is always some kid that may be seeing me for the first or last time. I owe him my best.

Joe DiMaggio (1914–1999)
New York Yankees

Joltin' Joe Said:

ON OPENING DAY: You look forward
to it like a birthday party when
you're a kid. You think something
wonderful is going to happen.

Joe DiMaggio (1914–1999)
New York Yankees

I came up twice in a game with the bases
loaded and both times I hit balls into
the alley, four hundred fifty feet away.
Home runs in any other park. Well, each
time my brother robbed me by making
catches on the warning track. Instead
of a possible eight RBI, or at least five
or six, I got nothing. That night Dom
[DiMaggio] came over to my place for
dinner. I remember letting him in the door
and then not speaking to him until we
were almost done eating. I was that mad.

Joe DiMaggio (1914–1999)
New York Yankees

A ball player has got to be kept
hungry to become a big leaguer.
That is why no boy from a rich
family ever made the big leagues.

Joe DiMaggio (1914–1999)
New York Yankees

I thank the good Lord for
making me a Yankee.

Joe DiMaggio (1914–1999)
New York Yankees

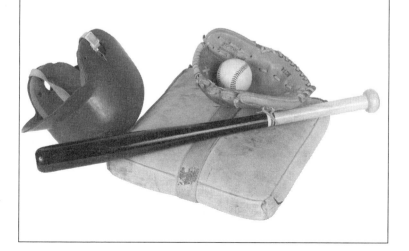

The Truth about Baseball

Baseball is a game of race, creed,
and color. The race is to first base.
The creed is the rules of the game.
The color? Well, the home team
wears white uniforms and the
visiting team wears gray.

Joe Garagiola (1926–)
*St. Louis Cardinals, Pittsburgh Pirates, Chicago Cubs,
New York Giants, sports broadcaster*

It's a mere moment in a man's
life between the all-star game
and the old-timers' game.

Vin Scully (1927–)
Sportscaster, voice of the Los Angeles Dodgers

I don't want to play golf.
When I hit a ball, I want
someone else to go chase it.

Rogers Hornsby (1896–1963)
St. Louis Cardinals

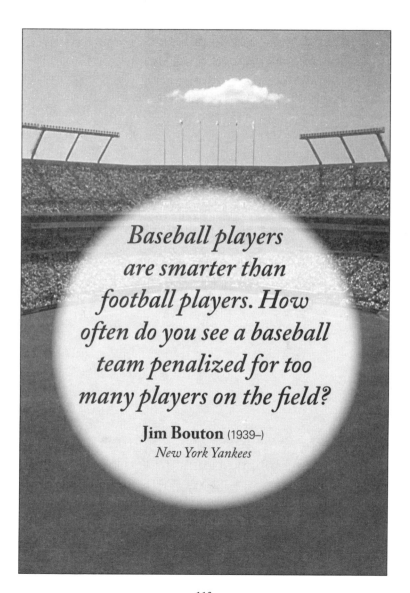

Baseball players are smarter than football players. How often do you see a baseball team penalized for too many players on the field?

Jim Bouton (1939–)
New York Yankees

When you say you're a Padre, people ask: When did you become a parent? When you say you're a Cardinal, they tell you to work hard because the next step is pope. But when you say you're a Dodger, everybody knows you're in the Major Leagues.

Tommy Lasorda (1927–)
Manager, Los Angeles Dodgers

Say this much for the big league baseball—it is beyond question the greatest conversation piece ever invented in America.

Bruce Catton (1899–1978)
Historian

Perhaps the truest axiom in baseball is that the toughest thing to do is repeat.

Walter Alston (1911–1984)
Manager, Los Angeles Dodgers

Baseball is dull only
to dull minds.

Red Barber (1908–1992)
Sportscaster, Voice of the Reds,
Brooklyn Dodgers, New York Yankees

Baseball is a game where
a curve is an optical illusion,
a screwball can be a pitch or a
person, stealing is legal, and you
can spit anywhere you like except in
the umpire's eye or on the ball.

Jim Murray (1919–1998)
Sports columnist, Los Angeles Times

You spend a good piece
of your life gripping a baseball,
and it turns out it was the other
way around all the time.

Jim Bouton (1939–)
New York Yankees

Fans don't boo nobodies.

Reggie Jackson (1946–)
Oakland Athletics, New York Yankees,
California Angels

A critic once characterized baseball
as six minutes of action crammed
into two and one-half hours.

Ray Fitzgerald
Sportswriter

If you step on people in this life, you're
going to come back as a cockroach.

Willie Davis (1940–)
Los Angeles Dodgers

Baseball is the only sport I know
when you're on the offense, the
other team controls the ball.

Ken Harrelson (1941–)
Kansas City Athletics, Boston Red Sox,
Cleveland Indians

Jimmy Connors plays two tennis matches and winds up with eight hundred fifty thousand dollars, and Muhammad Ali fights one bout and winds up with five million bucks. Me, I play one hundred ninety games—if you count exhibitions—and I'm overpaid.

Johnny Bench (1947–)
Cincinnati Reds

My high salary for one season was forty-six thousand dollars and a Cadillac.

Duke Snider (1926–)
Los Angeles Dodgers

The difference between the old ballplayer and the new ballplayer is the jersey. The old ballplayer cared about the name on the front. The new ballplayer cares about the name on the back.

Steve Garvey (1948–)
Los Angeles Dodgers,
four-time Gold Glove winner

Baseball is almost the only orderly thing in a very unorderly world. If you get three strikes, even the best lawyer in the world can't get you off.

Bill Veeck (1914–1987)
Baseball team owner

Twenty games is the magic figure for pitchers. Three hundred is the magic figure for batters. It pays off in salary and reputation. And those are the two things that keep a ballplayer in business.

Warren Spahn (1921–2003)
Milwaukee Braves, winningest left-handed pitcher of all time

Baseball is the only game left for people. To play basketball, you have to be seven feet, six inches. To play football, you have to have the same width.

Bill Veeck (1914–1987)
Baseball team owner

Any time you think you have
the game conquered the game
will turn around and punch
you right in the nose.

Mike Schmidt (1949-)
Philadelphia Phillies

Baseball is the belly of society.
Straighten out baseball and you'll
straighten out the rest of the world.

Bill Lee (1946-)
Boston Red Sox

Every day is a new opportunity.
You can build on yesterday's success
or put its failures behind and start
over again. That's the way life is,
with a new game every day, and
that's the way baseball is.

Bob Feller (1918-)
Cleveland Indians

Ty Cobb

Elected to Hall of Fame	1936 (First inductee)
Main Position	Centerfield
Primary Team	Detroit Tigers

Ty Cobb held ninety major league records when he retired after the 1928 season. His skill as a hitter was almost overshadowed by his reputation as a fierce competitor—a reputation he encouraged.

When Ty left home as a young man to play baseball, his businessman father was dismayed, and said, "Don't come home a failure." Ty never did.

Joining the Detroit Tigers in 1907, he won nine consecutive batting titles, the youngest player to ever do so. Cobb studied pitchers and took advantage of their weaknesses. He trained relentlessly—practicing sliding until his legs were raw. He placed blankets along the base path and practiced bunting. During the winter he wore weighted boots to strengthen his legs. Cobb took every opportunity to gain an edge over his opponents, most of whom admired his drive to succeed.

Cobb may have been baseball's greatest player. His batting accomplishments are legendary—a lifetime average of .367; 297 triples; 4,191 hits; twelve batting titles; twenty-three straight seasons in which he hit over .300; three .400 seasons (topped by a .420 mark in 1911); and 2,245 runs. Intimidating the opposition, "The Georgia Peach" stole 892 bases during a twenty-four-year career primarily with the Detroit Tigers.

Cobb appreciated the value of a dollar and engaged in annual haggles with Detroit executives before signing his contract. Cobb's earnings were invested wisely and he became one of baseball's first millionaires.

Cobb will always be remembered as the player with the highest career batting average in baseball history.

Every great batter works on the
theory that the pitcher is more afraid
of him than he is of the pitcher.

Ty Cobb (1886–1961)
Detroit Tigers

Ty Said:

A ball bat is a wondrous weapon.

Ty Cobb (1886–1961)
Detroit Tigers

Baseball is a red-blooded sport for
red-blooded men. It's no pink tea,
and mollycoddles had better stay
out. It's a struggle for supremacy,
a survival of the fittest.

Ty Cobb (1886–1961)
Detroit Tigers

I had to fight all my life to survive. They
were all against me . . . but I beat the
bastards and left them in the ditch.

Ty Cobb (1886–1961)
Detroit Tigers

I never could stand losing. Second place
didn't interest me. I had a fire in my belly.

Ty Cobb (1886–1961)
Detroit Tigers

The trouble with baseball today is that most of the players are in the game for the money and that's it, not for the love of it, the excitement of it, the thrill of it.

Ty Cobb (1886–1961)
Detroit Tigers

The Media is the Message

I always turn to the sports
page first, which records people's
accomplishments. The front page
has nothing but man's failures.

Earl Warren (1891–1974)
Chief Justice, Supreme Court

It's a weird scene. You win a few
baseball games and all of a sudden
you're surrounded by reporters and
TV men with cameras asking you
about Vietnam and race relations.

Vida Blue (1949–)
Pitcher, Oakland Athletics

I know what the word "media"
means. It's plural for "mediocre."

Rocky Bridges (1927–)
Brooklyn Dodgers, Cincinnati Reds

By the Numbers

Statistics are to baseball what flaky
crust is to Mom's apple pie.

Harry Reasoner (1923–1991)
Newscaster

Baseball isn't statistics—baseball
is DiMaggio rounding second.

Jimmy Cannon (1910–1973)
Sportswriter

Awards mean a lot, but they don't
say it all. The people in baseball
mean more to me than statistics.

Ernie Banks (1931–)
Chicago Cubs

Baseball statistics are like a girl in a bikini.
They show a lot, but not everything.

Toby Harrah (1948–)
Cleveland Indians

Hank Aaron

Elected to Hall of Fame	1982
Main Position	Right Field
Primary Team	Milwaukee Braves

Hank Aaron, with his understated style and powerful wrists, became the all-time home run champion with 755.

He began his career by playing semi-pro ball at fifteen, and playing shortstop for two seasons with the Indianapolis Clowns in the Negro Leagues. Aaron became their first African-American player when he joined the Braves in 1954. Two years later he won his first batting title. In 1959 he won a second batting title with a .355 average and led the league in slugging with a .636 average.

In 1971 Aaron had a career-high .669 average and hit forty-seven home runs to climb to third place on the all-time list with 639. Two years later, he hit forty home runs, the most ever by a player his age. And finally in 1974 he surpassed Babe Ruth's record for home runs.

Aaron had one of the most consistent offensive careers in baseball history. In addition to 755 home runs, he holds the major league record for total bases, extra-base hits, and RBIs. Aaron was named the 1957 National League MVP, won three Gold Gloves for his play in right field, and was named to a record twenty-four All-Star squads.

I never doubted my ability, but when you hear all your life you're inferior, it makes you wonder if the other guys have something you've never seen before. If they do, I'm still looking for it.

Hank Aaron (1934–)
Atlanta Braves

You can only milk a cow so long, then you're left holding the pail.

Hank Aaron (1934–)
Atlanta Braves

Hammering Hank Said:

I would like people not to think in terms
of the 755 home runs I hit but think in
terms of what I've accomplished off the
field and some of the things I stood for.

Hank Aaron (1934–)
Atlanta Braves

There is no logical reason why girls
shouldn't play baseball; it's not that tough.

Hank Aaron (1934–)
Atlanta Braves

Looking at the ball going over
the fence isn't going to help.

Hank Aaron (1934–)
Atlanta Braves

I don't see pitches down the middle
anymore . . . not even at batting practice.

Hank Aaron (1934–)
Atlanta Braves

My motto was always to
keep swinging. Whether I was
in a slump or feeling badly or
having trouble off the field, the
only thing to do was keep swinging.

Hank Aaron (1934–)
Atlanta Braves

The pitcher has got only
a ball. I've got a bat. So the
percentage of weapons is in my
favor and I let the fellow with
the ball do the fretting.

Hank Aaron (1934–)
Atlanta Braves

The triple is the most exciting
play in baseball. Home runs win
a lot of games, but I never understood
why fans are so obsessed with them.

Hank Aaron (1934–)
Atlanta Braves

It took me seventeen years to get three thousand hits in baseball. I did it all in one afternoon on the golf course.

Hank Aaron (1934–)
Atlanta Braves

INDEX

A

Aaron, Hank 22, 27, 95, 126, 127, 128, 129, 130
Adcock, Joe 72
Alston, Walter 22, 114
Anderson, Larry 50
Anderson, Sparky 21
Arthur, Chester A. 32

B

Banks, Ernie 18, 125
Barber, Red 115
Barry, Dave 54
Barzun, Jacques Martin 1
Bench, Johnny 48, 99, 117
Berra, Yogi 100, 102
Blue, Vida 124
Bogart, Humphrey 97
Bouton, Jim 75, 113, 115
Brett, George 90
Bridges, Rocky 124
Burdett, Lew 69
Bush, George W. 29, 34

C

Campanella, Roy 9
Cannizzaro, Chris 98
Cannon, Jimmy 125
Cartwright, Alexander 2
Cash, Norm 71

Catton, Bruce 114
Clemente, Roberto 15
Clinton, Bill 26
Cobb, Ty 90, 120, 121, 122, 123
Colavito, Rocky 18

D

Dark, Alvin 97
Davis, Willie 116
Dean, Dizzy 73, 75
Dickey, Bill 98
Diller, Phyllis 48
DiMaggio, Joe 38, 108, 109, 110, 111
Doubleday, Abner 2
Drysdale, Don 67
Durocher, Leo 16, 18, 20, 69, 84

E

Eisenhower, Dwight D. 32, 35

F

Feller, Bob 14, 73, 119
Fitzgerald, Ray 116
Ford, Gerald 33
Ford, Whitey 68
Fox, Nellie 68, 89
Foxworthy, Jeff 53
Foxx, Jimmie 90

G

Garagiola, Joe 47, 112
Garvey, Steve 117
Gehrig, Lou 80
Gibson, Bob 14, 15, 71, 75
Goetz, Larry 82
Gomez, Lefty 90
Gumbel, Bryant 60

H

Harrah, Toby 125
Harrelson, Ken 116
Herzog, Whitey 16, 21
Hoover, Herbert 34
Hornsby, Rogers 58, 112
Hubbard, Elbert 60

J

Jackson, Reggie 116
John, Tommy 73
Jupiter, Harry 30

K

Killebrew, Harmon 8
Klem, Bill 58, 82, 83
Koufax, Sandy 76, 77
Kubek, Tony 96

L

Larsen, Don 55
Lasorda, Tommy 17, 19, 21, 23, 114
Lee, Bill 119
Lemon, Bob 73
Lieberman, Joe 9
Luciano, Ron 82, 84

M

Mack, Connie 61
Mantle, Mickey 86, 88, 92, 93, 94, 95, 96
Maris, Roger 86, 88
Martin, Billy 20
Mathews, Eddie 9
Mays, Willie 28, 29, 30, 31
McCarver, Tim 75
McGwire, Mark 6
Murray, Jim 70, 115
Musial, Stan 7, 46, 91

N

Nixon, Richard 33
Norman, Al 83

P

Paige, Satchel 62, 63, 64, 65, 75, 91
Posada, Jorge 98
Povich, Shirley 55

R

Reagan, Ronald 34
Reasoner, Harry 125
Reese, Pee Wee 89
Rizzuto, Phil 49
Robinson, Frank 56, 57
Robinson, Jackie 5, 24, 26
Roosevelt, Franklin 33
Rose, Pete 15, 60
Rosen, Al 89
Ruth, Babe 4, 10, 11, 12, 13

S

Schmidt, Mike 119
Scully, Vin 112
Sharon, Dick 78
Simon, Roger 97
Slaughter, Enos 7
Smith, Red 105
Snider, Duke 117
Sosa, Sammy 6
Spahn, Warren 19, 69, 79, 118
Stargell, Willie 60
Steinberg, Saul 6
Stengel, Casey 15, 20, 21, 22, 48,
    50, 98, 99
Switzer, Barry 107

T

Thompson, Fresco 30
Thomson, Bobby 104, 105
Truman, Harry 32

U

Uecker, Bob 99

V

Vander Meer, Johnny 66
Veeck, Bill 59, 118

W

Warren, Earl 124
Weaver, Earl 16, 18, 20, 71, 84
Westrum, Wes 58
Williams, Ted 36, 38, 39
Wilson, Hack 63

Y

Yastrzemski, Carl 14, 59

SOURCES

Baseball Almanac
> baseball-almanac.com/quoimenu.shtml

Creative Baseball
> creativebaseball.com

Quotations for Creative Thinking
> creativequotations.com

Baseball quotes—ThinkExist quotations
> en.thinkexist.com/quotations/baseball

Famous Baseball Quotations
> woodbridgefbl.com/famous_baseball_quotations.htm

quoteland.com

Favorite Quotations—Baseball—Ideas to motivate, educate
> dailycelebrations.com/baseball.htm

Baseball quotes for fans
> love-quotes-and-quotations.com/baseball-quotes.html

The Physics of Baseball by Porter Johnson
> iit.edu/-johnsonp/smart00/lesson3.htm

quotegarden.com/baseball.html

Baseball World/Baseball Quotes Archive
> geocities.com/colosseum/park/1138/quotes/quotes.html

sportsquotations.com

Yahoo Sports

Baseball Quotes by Baseball Almanac

Life quotes—Famous Life Quotations
> Home.attnet/-quotations/life.html

ABOUT THE AUTHOR

Margaret Queen has been a baseball fan all of her life. She played varsity softball for four years in high school, was a high school physical education teacher, taught and coached softball, and was a certified umpire.

She has an M.A. degree in physical education from the University of California, Santa Barbara. Margaret lives with her husband in Tennessee and has two grown children and one grandchild.

Margaret is the author of *So You're Off to Summer Camp: A Trunk Load of Tips for a Fun-Filled Camp Adventure, One Hundred Years of Women's Wisdom*, and *Baby Tips for Moms and Dads*.